Poverty Deserved?
Relieving the Poor
in Victorian Liverpool

Anthony Miller

Illustrations acknowledgements

Sincere thanks to the following for permission to reproduce illustrations:

Liverpool City Libraries - frontispiece, 1, 2, 3, 5, 6, 7, 8, 9, 10, 11, 12, 13, 14, 15, 16 17.

Liverpool City Engineers Department - 4

First published 1988 by Liver Press, 1 & 3 Grove Road, Rock Ferry, Birkenhead, Merseyside L42 3XS.

Copyright © Anthony Miller, 1988.
Printed by Birkenhead Press Limited, 1 & 3 Grove Road, Rock Ferry, Birkenhead, Merseyside L42 3XS.
ISBN

Contents

For my daughters
Lisa and Loren
with love

Preface

Historian G. M. Trevelyan described social history as 'history of the people with the politics taken out'. This social history concerns the people in the poor community of Victorian Liverpool. It is an account of the severe harshness of poverty in the city and how the poor encountered it in the days before the modern Welfare State. The study incorporates a consideration of the men and women of the leading charitable organisations. These people played an important role in the lives of the poor, for they believed poverty could be adequately dealt with by voluntary philanthropic effort. This concept crucially affected the lives of many poor families in Victorian Livepool. The methods and attitudes of the charitable institutions of the day produced circumstances as may well have been deemed 'as cold as charity'.

I should like to express my sincere thanks to a number of people who have given me help and advice in writing this book. I must acknowledge my gratitude to Sam Davies, of Liverpool Polytechnic School of Humanities, for his guidance and help with the initial research. I am very grateful to Eric Taplin, David Kermode and Pat Ayers for their kindly criticisms and valuable suggestions on the content of the original manuscript. The staff of Liverpool City Record Office have been most co-operative and have kindly placed much material at my disposal, during my search for primary sources and documentation. I thank Ian Qualtrough and Susan Yee of the Photographic Unit at Liverpool University for the excellent work they have done. Thanks also go to Patricia McMillan and Dianne Murgatroyd for typing the manuscript and to Val Taylor and Jacqueline Bracken for typesetting and design . Finally, special thanks go to my wife Carol for her constant support and patient encouragement throughout.

Rag market c. 1895. Photograph by T. Burke

Chapter One

IN THE WORKHOUSE

The last thirty to forty years have proved to be a very fruitful period for the study of social history and a great deal of research has been carried out into the question of poverty and its relief in nineteenth century Britain. The evidence suggests that Victorian Britain, at that time the richest and most powerful nation in the world, displayed a facade that concealed some of the most appalling social and environmental conditions imaginable. Behind the splendid architecture of the Victorian city there existed a continuing drama that involved the struggle for life itself. The Victorian city was, quite simply, a lethal place to live in.

The aim of this study is to investigate and examine poverty and, perhaps more importantly, the efforts to alleviate poverty in what has been generally regarded as one of the worst examples of the lethal Victorian city, Liverpool, where the available statistics on mortality rates show that the chance of poor residents reaching old age were drastically minimised. Statistics reveal that in 1847 the average duration of life in Liverpool, an urban-industrial area, was a mere twenty years five months while in a rural town, such as Ulverston in North Lancashire, it was forty one years eight months.[1]

Dr. Duncan, Liverpool's and the country's first Public Medical Officer, stated in the 1840s that Liverpool was the most unhealthy town in England and modern historians such as Margaret Simey and David Owen both regard Liverpool as *the* worst example of the shameful Victorian city. Poverty was more desperate, housing more squalid, the state of public health more shocking and social distinctions more cruel than perhaps anywhere else in the country.

The first part of this study concentrates on city life. After a short survey of commercial and demographic expansion, the appalling poverty which affected the poor is analysed. What was their social and economic position in society? What were the causes of povety? Was drink a major problem, and if so, was it a cause of the poor's condition or did their condition cause them to drink? An analytical study of the occupational structure follows to identify just who the poor were, including the prevalence and importance of the casual labour market in Liverpool.

1

Part two examines the reasons why chronic poverty survived all attempts to eradicate it. In 1896, William Grisewood,[2] the Secretary of the Central Relief Society (C.R.S.) in Liverpool, admitted that the problem of removing poverty and suffering remained 'as great as ever' after nearly 40 years of effort. The private charities of Victorian Liverpool will come under the microscope, and we shall examine critically the philanthropists, their institutions and their methods and attitudes towards the poor and to poor relief in general. It shall become clear that the State acted only in cases of severe hardship via the 1834 Poor Law, which was ill-equipped to cope with the enormous problems of urban, industrial society. Poverty was a vast social problem that could only be tackled effectively by massive state intervention. However, it was not until the turn of the century, after the response to the publication of the reports of Charles Booth and Seebohm Rowntree on poverty in London and York respectively, where their statistical evidence confirmed that the problem of poverty was far beyond the scope of private charitable benevolence, that public awareness of the actual extent of the problem was finally shaken out of its lethargy and attitudes began to change.

Although the study is critical of the Poor Law and private charities, there is much evidence to suggest a genuine faith and determination for the care and benefaction of the poor. The selfless devotion of some exceptional men and women throughout the period must not be overlooked. Yet they were easily outweighed by other 'devotees' who were obsessed with the Victorian attitudes towards poverty, of moral failure, self-help and individualism, and respectability. The opinion of many middle-class observers was that the lot of the poor was not the consequence of poverty, but of that which creates poverty, that is improvidence, indolence and, most of all, intemperance. Efforts were generally directed towards the betterment of the individual while the social surroundings, for example, the deplorable housing conditions and the state of public health, were largely neglected. G.D.H. Cole[3] made the point admirably when he argued that the Victorian philanthropist's weakness... 'was that with all his ready sympathy, he looked much less at causes than at effects, and never penetrated below the surface ills of the society which he so ardently desired to reform.'

Perhaps the real motives of other philanthropists were rather less than sympathetic. There was evidence of fraud, snobbery and simple ambition amongst some donors. In 1860 The Times[4] noted that a new form of criminal had appeared in correlation with the great mid-century increase in the number of charitable organisations that were being established throughout Britain. This felon devoted years to... 'acquiring episcopal smiles while quietly misappropriating the charities' funds' and in those early years before any centralised bodies such as the CRS in Liverpool (1863) and the Charity

Organisation Society (COS) in London (1869)[5] were established the clear opportunities to resort to fraud must have been very tempting to the less honest secretary. Snobbery and ambition were, perhaps, even more important to others, as charitable activity could be a means of attaining social mobility. Margaret Simey[6] points out that . . . 'through the subscription list of a charity one could display one's wealth to public view, co-operate openly with the aristocracy and thus buy a place in public life or even a seat in Parliament.' Charitable activity could often be of more benefit to the giver than to the recipient providing opportunities for social climbing.

On a similar note Brian Harrison[7] has argued that many philanthropists preferred to see the effects of their donations in their own localities rather than in the slum areas where aid was most needed but which the wealthy 'were often too fastidious or frightened to visit'. William Booth cynically highlighted this in his *In Darkest England and the Way Out*, which was purposely meant to relate to Stanley's *In Darkest Africa* which had been published in the same year (1890). Booth had encountered many slum areas in the cities which housed large numbers of people in deplorable poverty but whom the majority of the upper and middle-classes knew absolutely nothing about. There was a decided lack of public awareness in Liverpool. The satirical weekly magazine *Porcupine*, which was published in the second-half of the century, conducted a seventeen week survey of the slum areas of Liverpool entitled 'The Mysteries of the Courts'[8] which graphically described the conditions that the poor lived in. In one account Porcupine investigators walked through No. 2 Court Hockenhall Alley off Dale Street and found that three houses were inhabited by no less than 50 persons, the W.C. was choked, heaps of rubbish stood in corners, there were filled ashpits and the stench was described as 'poisonous'. But *Porcupine* argued that 'the more comfortable portion of the public of Liverpool knew nothing about such scenes'. The article went on. 'Probably not one in a hundred of them has ever been in one of those places much less noted the regular gradation from lowest depths to lower still'.

Derek Fraser[9] has put forward another possible factor that inspired philanthropists to encourage charitable activity. He argues that underlying much Victorian willingness to support charitable enterprises was a genuine and persistent fear of social revolution. Social tension in the Victorian period was never far below the surface, and contrary to the conventional belief in the placidity of mid and late Victorian society, it surfaced on a number of occasions. In order to prevent an assault on the whole basis of society and the division of wealth within it men were prepared to siphon off some of their wealth for use by those in need. As Gladstone reminded a critic of his policies. "Please recollect that we have got to govern millions of hard hands; that it must be done by force, fraud or goodwill; that the latter has been tried and is answering".

Yet whatever the motives of the nineteenth-century philanthropist the underlying theme of the popular political economy of the day saw, above all else, individual effort to be the way in which the whole society gained. The ambitious, gifted and hard-working could make it to the top positions in society if they believed in thrift, self-denial and other middle-class virtues that were concerned with respectability. As Simey argues 'a man's first duty was a matter he alone could decide'. Poverty was avoidable through personal initiative and the more difficult it became to comprehend and treat the problem, the more inclined were the middle-classes to attribute poverty to failings in the characters of the poor themselves. The Central Relief Society, and men like Grisewood in Liverpool, adhered to this opinion for they classified the poor into 'deserving' and 'undeserving' families or individuals. Yet how they reached a conclusion on who fell into which category was another matter. That was decided by visitors and caseworkers who were rigorous and strict in their enquiries. We shall examine these points in greater detail later.

No. 1   *Elderly vegetable seller c. 1890.* Photograph by C.F. Inston.

4

The remainder of this introductory chapter is devoted to a summary of that watershed of nineteenth century social policy; the 1834 Poor Law. The New Poor Law is the logical starting point in any discussion of nineteenth century poverty.

The two principal themes of the New Poor Law were concerned with 'indoor relief' and 'less eligibility'. The old allowance system was abolished and with it all outdoor relief for the able-bodied and their families. If people needed support from the state then it was to be provided in institutions, that is the workhouses, rather than in their homes or communities. Workhouses were purposely made into harsh, disciplined and unpleasant establishments, the idea being that people would not seek help unless really desperate. They were made 'less eligible'. If idleness was made more unpleasant than work, people would find work and there would be no destruction of the work ethic.

It is clear that the object of the new system was to discourage pauperism and not to eradicate the root causes of poverty. Edwin Chadwick, who had emerged as a public figure on his appointment as Secretary to the Commissioners of the Poor Law, hoped the new system would intimidate the 'undeserving' poor, restore the principle of work and independence and inculcate a sense of pride in the labourer's work. His conclusions implied that most pauperism was wilful and that the Poor Law would become a powerful stimulus to self-help. But the workhouse became a feared and stigmatized establishment. Many were regarded as worse than prisons. The insufficient diets, the separation of families according to sex and the constant incarceration of the inmates earned them an odious reputation among the working classes. Karl Marx described the workhouses of the New Poor Law as "the revenge of the borgeoisie upon the poor who appeal to its charity ... because pauperism was seen as a crime to be suppressed and punished". People were being treated often worse than criminals when their only crime was being unfortunate enough to be poor.

Michael Murphy was indicated that the Poor Law was ill-adapted to deal with urban industrial poverty and it was in the new industrial towns where the most dreadful conditions of poverty could be seen. He reaffirmed that the Commissioners were 'primarily concerned with pauperism, the allowance system and rural unemployment'. The 1834 system never worked effectively primarily because of the fear and stigma attached to the workhouse itself, but also because of the obvious contradictions in the Act. For example, in times of mass unemployment it was physically impossible to cater for everyone at or below the poverty line in the workhouse. Outdoor relief, and help and support from the community in the shape of neighbours and relatives, had to continue in some form, thus, defeating the object of integral indoor relief. Neighbours and relatives in the slum areas of Liverpool often banded together in times of crisis, with the celebrated 'whip round' a common feature.

The yawning gap between the mechanics of state and the poor community was occupied by what Derek Fraser called the 'torrent of charity' that rained down upon the poor in the mid-century years.

In Part Two of the study we shall examine the effects and range of this charity in Victorian Liverpool. But first we must turn our attention to the examination of poverty in the city. In many ways it is an account of life at its lowest, and most shocking levels.

NOTES AND REFERENCES

1. (From Tables published by the Health of Towns Assocation 1847) *Condition of Liverpool*, analysis of the Present Population Part VIII, p. 24. Canon A. Hume.

2. *Central Relief Society Annual Report 1896*, W. Grisewood.

3. G. D. H. Cole, *Chartist Portraits* (Macmillan 1941), p. 186. Cole was referring to Joseph Sturge in this particular passage.

4. Cited by Brian Harrison in an article entitled *Victorian Philanthropy*, Volume G, *Victorian Studies 1965-66* p. 364. Quoted in *The Times* 2 January 1860.

5. Liverpool - Central Relief Society founded in 1863 extended its name in 1871 to the Central Relief and Charity Organisation Society. But to avoid any unnecessary confusion with the Charity Organisation Society of London, which was founded in 1869, we shall continue to refer to the former as the CRS.

6. M. B. Simey *Charitable effort in Liverpool* (Liverpool University Press 1951) p. 56.

7. B. Harrison 'Victorian Philanthropy', p. 367. Quote from Henry Solly, *These Eighty Years* (London 1893) II, 237.

8. *The 'Porcupine'* - Hugh Shimmin (Ed.), a journal of current events, social, political and stirical. 'The Mysteries of the Courts', a series of seventeen chapters published from November 15th 1862 to March 21st 1863. Our quote was taken from CHAPTER XIII 14th February 1863.

9. D. Fraser - *The Evolution of the British Welfare State* - A History of Social Policy since the Industrial Revolution (2nd edition Macmillan 1984), p. 117.

Chapter Two

NEW WEALTH...NEW POOR AND NEW HOVELS

In order to explain the particular social and economic character of the Liverpool poor, and the nature and effects of the casual labour problem it is necessary to survey the commercial and demographic foundations of the town. For the conditions which gave rise to the chronic poverty of our period were not brought about by accident. They originated from the expansion which radically changed the character of Liverpool in the late eighteenth and early nineteenth centuries. Physical growth was accompanied by rapid population growth but it was not matched by a commensurable expansion in administration and regulation, or by the consideration of unscrupulous landowners and builders, who simply crowded as many people as possible into the court and cellar dwellings that were springing up in the centre of the town. Land became a scarce and valuable commodity that was used to its maximum efficiency but the cost of which was measured by human suffering on a large scale.

Liverpool's motto, which was adopted by the merchants on the town council in the early eighteenth century, - *Deus notis haec otia jecit* ("God has made for us this ease")[1] emphasises the town's geographical situation which made it a convenient centre and outlet for both the export of northern English products, such as South Lancashire coal and Cheshire rock salt, and the import of goods from the colonies, notably in those early years, Virginian tobacco and West Indian sugar. Of course a third element of this early colonial trade was slaves, and the fact that Liverpool merchants had already been trading with the West Indies made the triangular trade in human cargo between Liverpool, the West Indies and the West African coast an easy and lucrative venture. Although there were communication links inland, mostly by expensive and inefficient road and pack horse tracks, it is clear that in this early period Liverpool's main prosperity and growth was essentially linked with the water. By 1730 her contacts with these were being augmented by the navigation of the Mersey, the Irwell and other rivers around her natural location which established the first water connections with Manchester and with the coal and salt we have just mentioned. Later in the century the systematic development of artificial waterways, such as the Sankey, Grand

Trunk, Bridgewater, and Leeds-Liverpool canals, established further connections with nearly all the major industrial areas of England and placed Liverpool in a position to become the main distribution centre for many of the goods produced in the industrial heartland.

No. 2 *George's Dock Passage; Mann island on the left. c. 1890.* Photograph by C.F. Inston.

Added to the improvement in communications inland, foreign and colonial trade also improved rapidly in the second-half of the eighteenth century. The number and tonnage of ships increased appreciably and Liverpool's first two docks the 'Old Dock' built in 1715, and Salthouse Dock, 1734 were supplemented by the development of new docks. By 1825 there were seven wet docks in port, and by 1857 a further 21 had been added, with most built under the supervision of engineer Jesse Hartley. The following table shows the remarkable progress of the shipping of Liverpool in comparison with the two other major British ports, London and Hull, in the first half of the nineteenth century.

Table I

Vessels and tonnage of the three principal ports of Great Britain in 1850 as compared with 1816

	1816		1850	
	Total Ships	Total Tonnage	Total Ships	Total Tonnage
Liverpool	2946	642,063	9338	3,262,253
London	6196	1,247,873	16437	3,289,631
Hull	1185	185,331	4249	836,173

Source: Return of vessels and tonnage August 1851 Custom House London.[2]

The line of docks that extended both north and south from the Pier Head, to Bootle and Toxteth respectively, placed Liverpool alongside London as one of the major ports in the world. The structure of the nineteenth century Liverpool economy was built around the trade and commerce that flowed in and out of those docks. For although there were some manufacturing industries of minor importance in Liverpool in the late eighteenth century, such as pottery at the famous Herculaneum works[3] and watchmaking, they declined rapidly in the nineteenth century. Liverpool was, a commercial, not an industrial society. The leading men of the town were merchants rather than industrialists, and this fact may go some way towards explaining the wide social distinction which occurred among the different classes in Liverpool society and, perhaps, to the lack of awareness about the extent of poverty that we described earlier. As Simey has pointed out, whereas in other industrial towns there was a certain homogeneity of life centring on the mill or the factory, Liverpool's mercantile character denied her this connection, and, as a contemporary of the period commented

> "In Liverpool almost alone amongst provincial cities . . . the intercourse between master and men and between employer and employed ceases on payment of wages. This is a desolate condition of honest striving industry and bodes no good to the social system".[4]

Despite this situation people still, however, flocked to Liverpool in their thousands. It became the boom city of the period with population growth matched to commercial growth. As statistics reveal, the two were closely tied:

Table II

The rise of trade and population in 19th Century Liverpool

	Shipping 000s Tons	Population 000s
* 1800	450.0	77
+ 1830	1412.0	190
1850	3289.6	360
1870	5728.5	530

Sources:
* Cotton and Mountford, *Story of Liverpool*, p.46
+ I. C. Taylor, *Blackspot on the Mersey*, pp. 12-13. (Shipping — Hyde, 1971, Appendix i. Population — Table A3.1).

Therefore, an ever-increasing army of hands was needed to cope with the expansion and the town became a magnet for many displaced persons from Ireland, Wales, Scotland and counties which bordered the Irish Sea, such as

No. 3 *Canning Dock c.1890.* Photograph by C.F. Inston.

Lancashire, Cheshire and Cumberland. They were attracted by the unskilled and casual nature of employment which became one of the dominant characteristics of Liverpool's nineteenth century society, and is of great significance to the understanding of the town's urban structure. Michael Rose has noted that of all the causes of poverty in nineteenth century Britain the most prominent resulted from 'the receipt of inadequate and irregular earnings'.[5] There seems no doubt that the prevalence of casual and unskilled labour in Liverpool accentuated this problem condemning a large proportion of the increased population to extreme standards of povety and hardship.

This poverty would be reflected in the abysmal environmental and social conditions in the city. By the 1840's Liverpool had the inevitable reputation of being the unhealthiest town in the kingdom. Her mortality rates are higher than in other major English cities as the following table shows:

Table III

**Mortality rates of seven principle towns in England —
average annual rate 1838**

Liverpool	34.8
Manchester	33.7
Bristol	30.9
Sheffield	30.4
Leeds	27.2
Birmingham	27.2
Metropolis	26.7
*1838-42	

Source: Duncan — Parliamentary papers. 1844 XVII (on the physical causes of the high rate of mortality in Liverpool. Evidence to Commission on State of Large Towns and Populus Districts). First Report, p.124-125.

The poor were housed in conditions probably unequalled anywhere else and the concentration of people, in relation to ground area, was unparalleled by any other large town. In 1844, Liverpool's population density measured 140,000 persons per square mile, which exceeded that of Manchester, London or Leeds.[6] Indeed, at ward level, the situation could be even worse. Duncan noted, in particular, that the Vauxhall and Exchange wards, which were the main reception areas for immigrants, afforded "examples of a greater

11

concentration of inhabitants than existed in any English town". One of the worst streets, Lace St. had only four square yards per inhabitant!

The area around Tithebarn St. and Great Crosshall St. provided the nucleus from which a good deal of the overcrowding occurred. Court and cellar dwellings which had already been built in the area at the beginning of the nineteenth century, on land sold by the Cross estate, were extended. The new owners purposely covered the area with a dense mass of court property, ingeniously arranged to maximise the number of houses at the least possible cost. In these court areas, a small area of ground of about thirty to forty feet wide, was wholly or partly surrounded by walls or buildings of appreciable height, which served to shut out the very light of day for most residents. With this cul de sac arrangement, access to the court was gained through a narrow passage with usually one communal water tap in the middle and one or two communal toilets at the end of the court. Often toilets would be in disrepair or choked for lack of water supply, making the conditions and atmosphere both noxious and very unhealthy. Although efforts were made, most notably by the Sanitary Act of 1846, to remedy some of the defects of the law relating to

No. 4 *Clearing blocked sewers in a north end court. c. 1890s.*

the layout of such accommodation, unscrupulous landlords had the opportunity to hurriedly construct another thousand courts, before the Act could be implemented. Indeed, although the authorities continued to take action to demolish or close these properties, some court and cellar dwellings, particularly in the Scotland Road area, survived well into the twentieth century.

Liverpool's population increased even more rapidly after the Famine Migration from Ireland in 1846/47. In one three-month period from January to April 1847, an astonishing 127,850 Irish people arrived in the port.[7] Many moved on but a significant number stayed. Consequently, the poor were increasingly confined to an ever-decreasing stock of cheap, insanitary and overcrowded dwellings. The cheap housing stock was further reduced by demolition in other parts of the town, to facilitate further commercial expansion and development. Between 1847 and 1850, for example, railway extension gobbled up houses and land in the neighbourhood of Victoria Street, Lime Street and Skelhorne Street and it was the poorest members of the community who suffered. The clearances further isolated them and drove them into ghettos.

Unlike the skilled artisans and the lower middle-classes, who were moving away to new housing in the suburbs of Everton and Toxteth Park, the unskilled casual workforce, who constituted the vast majority of waterfront workers had to stay in close proximity to their places of work. There was a lack of cheap transport facilities. Personal contact was important in obtaining unskilled work and the means of obtaining information about employment opportunities would not be so forthcoming in the suburbs. The existence of street markets in the city centre meant that food was cheaper. Good credit relations with a landlord or a local shop could be established. There was also a reluctance to break with the sense of community forged between relatives, friends and neighbours. These factors explain why the unskilled casual was compelled to restrict his mobility. The gulf between the better off and the poor, or what may be best described as the 'donor and recipient' became even wider.

The Irish, especially, were very gregarious and tended to congregate in certain localities and in individual court houses which were often sub-let room by room or even part-room by part-room. Some of the streets in the lower quarters of the city were notorious for their deplorable conditions. The key problem was a lack of basic amenities, such as water supply, drainage and sewerage. It was the lack of these services to the court, rather than the actual house itself, which caused the cholera epidemics of 1932, 1849, 1854 and 1866. Cholera took a heavy toll of life in each epidemic e.g. the 1849 epidemic claimed 6,394 deaths, and in the 1866 epidemic in the short period from July

13

No. 5 *Back of St. John's market, Liverpool city centre c. 1890.* Photograph by C.F. Inston.

1st to July 13th alone, 1,762 deaths were recorded.[9] Some accounts of the apathy and the ignorance of cholera make grim reading. In the 1866 epidemic for example a Mrs. Boyle of No. 2 Court Bispham Street, a house in one of the worst slum districts which had many open cess-pools in its vicinity, was one of the first cases of cholera to be confirmed. Yet her husband and friends refused to bury the corpse and it was kept in the sitting room where 'men and women ate, drank and slept the orgies of the "wake"' ... and scores of people were maintained, amidst drunken and profane ribaldry, during the day and night'. Before the end of the month the dead women's husband and forty-eight other persons living within a short radius of the court had died from cholera. In another part of Stockdale Street, children were brought in turns to kiss and pat the corpse of a woman just dead from cholera. Within five days two of the children were dead.

Another killer was typhus fever. Heavy loss of life was recorded in 1847-48 and in the three years from 1863-6 a total of 5,275 deaths were recorded, i.e..

1863	1,165 registered deaths
1864	1,774 registered deaths
1865	2,336 registered deaths

14

Similarly, Duncan graphically described the squalor and misery that some people lived in, in his Annual Reports. He wrote in 1847:

"houses of the lowest class were so crowded that it was common to find every apartment of the dwelling occupied by several families. No curtain, no partition exists; no. separation of any kind can, in most of these cases, be practicable. The father, mother and children of one family sleep together in a corner; the father mother and children of another family sleep together in another; ditto, ditto, ditto, in a third etc. Sometimes there were beds upon stocks, but I have latterly seen more cases in which 'litters' are spread upon the floor or pavement, perhaps without any article of furniture in the apartment, or at most a broken chair or two, a log of wood or a stool".[11]

No. 6 *Number 2 Court, Sylvester Street*

The houses described had no constant water supply and little or no sewerage facilities. At best a court might share one or two 'privies', at worst the premises would be surrounded by filthy middens and cesspools. J. Finch wrote in 1842:

"I visited many families of this description...(breadwinner was unemployed)...in houses, rooms and cellars; the children almost in a

15

state of nudity, and it was impossible to look upon them without seeing hunger and starvation depicted in their countenances. Their habitations completely destitute of bedding, or any kind of furniture and sleeping on shavings or straw covered by a wrapper or a couple of sacks".[12]

H. Farrie wrote in 1886:

"The first house we entered was 10 house no. 2 court Fontenoy Street. The house is occupied by a man and four children. They have absolutely nothing, no light of any sort and no food ... by the flickering light of a match we see the 'home' of this wretched family. They are going to bed and the cellar door has been lifted off its hinges and laid down upon the floor of the room' ... this door acts as a bed for the children, the father having used his clothes to cover them then settles on a wooden box as ... there is nothing but the stone floor to lie down on and the room is absolutely bare of everything except for a small box which serves as his bed".[13]

The irony of these accounts is that the first (Duncan's) and the second (Finch's) were taken from reports that were completed in 1847 and 1842, respectively, while the third was from an article in the Liverpool Daily Post in 1886! Forty-four years lie between them yet the similarities suggest they might have been recorded on the same evening. The second and third accounts have other similarities; both were taken from the Vauxhall ward; both breadwinners were unskilled and, at the time, unemployed. Clearly they illustrate and provide the first indication of the ineffectiveness of the administrators of poor relief to ameliorate the poverty that existed.

This then was a sample of life in the poor community. Chronic poverty had become deeply rooted in this part of Liverpool society and presented a many-sided problem. What is more, the poor were becoming endlessly diversified as the causes of poverty were numerous. To low and irregular casual earnings can be added old age and infirmity, sickness and disablement, particularly when the breadwinner was struck down, the large family, the widow, the deserted wife and children, and the unemployed. Intemperance, indolence and sometimes sheer indifference to family obligations have also to be included yet not overstated. Grisewood[14] in a pamphlet on the causes of poverty, distinguished between those which depended on the poor themselves and those over which they had little or no control. He classified them into 'avoidable' causes the similarity between deserving and undeserving cases being obvious. Unavoidable causes were headed by 'irregularity of employment, followed by sickness, old age and seasonality'. (i.e. cyclical depression). Avoidable causes were headed by 'drink, laziness and a wasteful mode of life'. But, he allocated one and a half pages to unavoidable and four pages to avoidable causes, with intemperance his major concern.

The relationship between drink and poverty, which men like Grisewood regarded as so important, has to be seen in the context of the prevailing attitudes of the period. Nationally the most powerful force publicising the existence of self-inflicted poverty was the Temperance Movement. Prohibitionist groups such as the UK Alliance, were very influential in Victorian society in the second half of the century carrying the banners of virtue and respectability as their guides. Their organisations were dominated by self-made men overwhelmingly non-conformist, who upheld the principles and philosophy of self-help, thrift and hard work. They believed that the thriftless and drunken habits of the working classes were the primary cause of their predicament. It is true that by the mid 1870's drink consumption per head in Britain had reached unprecedented proportions and temperance writers Rowntree and Sherwell estimated that the typical working class family spent one-fifth of its annual income on alcohol.[15]

In Liverpool there were plenty of opportunities to resort to the temptations of alcohol. In 1858 a total of 1485 public houses existed in the Borough; which represented one to every 307 individuals. Indeed, in the district lying between Scotland Road and Vauxhall Road and extending from Great Crosshall Street in the south and Boundary Street in the north, Police registers show that no fewer than 158 fully-licensed houses, eight beerhouses and one off-licence were necessary to supply the drinking capabilities of the residents.[16] Some of the licensed premises gave no outward signs of their business. One public house frontage was a tobacconists shop and other bars could be entered by various doors from other streets and alleys in the warren of slums. One example shows that a drinking license applied to a bar registered in Fontenoy Street but two further doors in Great Crosshall Street gained people access to two separate bars which were strictly unlicensed.

Drunkenness in Liverpool achieved a degree unsurpassed anywhere in the U.K. and at its peak apprehensions for drunkenness per annum reached a ratio of 1 to 24 per head of population.[17] The following passage from *Porcupine* paints a vivid picture of the relationship between drink, brutality and poverty:

"Look at that grog-shop at the corner of Maguire Street. Look at that pale, shrivelled, dirty, ragged woman just leaving the door. Notice how her lips are parched—how her eyes glare—how her cheek is cut and the way her rags hang on her emaciated form. Now she lunges into the middle of the street and holding a quart bottle half-filled with ale in one hand and a jug in the other, she waves a triumphant defiance at some one up the street. But look by the kerb stone. See that little creature with curly hair, and its legs and face so caked with dirt and the flesh not

No. 7 *Children playing outside a street corner pub c. 1895.* Photograph by T. Burke.

discernible. Hear how piteously it cries because Mother is leaving it. Its hands are pressed against its eyes as it strives to cross the street to reach its mother, who is still waving the bottle and hurling imprecations on all sides. Poor little toddler—what life is opening up for thee?"[18]

This was the type of situation which shocked the temperance movement and which they so vehemently fought to eradicate. Yet they looked to the individual rather than to the environmental conditions for their answers. What has to be remembered is that places such as Maguire Street, in our example, were situated in the very heart of the worst examples of slum conditions, between Vauxhall Road and Scotland Road. So when one considers the overcrowded dwellings, the bad sanitary arrangements and the complete insecurity of people's lives it was perhaps inevitable that the poor would be brutalised and that they would seek to escape the dreadful monotony of their conditions of existence by turning to alcohol. It was cheap, there were plenty of opportunities to buy, with pubs and beer houses in abundance, and the warm hospitality they offered must have been a sore temptation when compared to the abject squalor of their own homes.

A further consideration is the relationship between the ruling class and drink. For there was another very powerful body in nineteenth century society, who occupied the opposite berth to the temperance movement; the brewers. Staunch financial supporters of the Tory Party, they held a good deal of political clout and this would be particularly noticeable in Liverpool, which politically, was overwhelmingly Tory up to 1945. In 1875 there were no less than sixty-five breweries in the city. It is clear their patrons would have made their presence felt in any efforts made by the temperance movement towards the reduction of drink consumption and/or public houses in the city.

Indications that the occupational structure was also a factor to consider were suggested by the Report from the Select Committee on Intemperance, which sat in 1878-9, when it remarked that 'the nature of the trade of manufacture in which the inhabitants are employed also tends to increase the habits of intemperance'.[19] The nature of the occupations on Liverpool's waterfront would have surely qualified on this score. Most jobs required considerable physical stamina and they bred a man who was trained by hard work and hard drinking, especially after a period of sustained labour which put money in his pocket and accelerated his thirst. Any study of poverty in the city would be incomplete without an understanding of the social and economic character of the Liverpool labour market. It is to this we now turn.

NOTES AND REFERENCES

1. Cotton and Mountford, *Story of Liverpool.* (A bound pamphlet printed in 1951 Liverpool University, available at County Record Office). The exact date of the adoption of the motto is unknown, but Cotton and Mountford put it at about 1725.

2. Thomas Baines, *History of Liverpool*, p. 825 (Baines 1852).

3. Liverpool had a long tradition of potting history, and there were about 25 potteries in Liverpool in the eighteenth century. The most famous—the Herculaneum Pottery Works was founded on the outskirts of the town and was situated in Toxteth Park from 1796-1840. See A. Smith, *Liverpool Herculaneum Pottery* (Barrie and Jenkins, London 1870).

4. William S. Trench M.O.H. *Workingmens Dwellings in Liverpool* (1897). Quoted in Simey *Charitable Effort* p. 12.

5. M. E. Rose, *Relief of Poverty, 1834-1914* (Macdonald 1972) (New Era) p. 17.

6. (Duncan 1844 p. 130 "On the physical causes of the high state of morality in Liverpool" p. 12-33). P. Papers 1844 XVIII. Cited in Taylor *Blackspot on the Mersey* p. 161.

7. *Liverpool Times*, April 20th 1847. Also in BAINES *Liverpool*, p. 678.

8. Railways in question were Lancashire and Yorkshire Railway and the London and North West Company's Railway.

9. T. H. Bickerton, *A Medical History of Liverpool from the Earliest Days to 1920*. (Ed. Bickerton HR. and Mackenna, RMG., Murray 1936).

10. Bickerton, *Medical History*, p. 179.

11. Duncan M.O.H. *Annual Report 1847*. Quoted in Simey *Charitable Effort*, p. 43.

12. J. Finch, *Statistics of Vauxhall Ward, Liverpool*, (1842), cited in Taylor *Blackspot*, p. 89.

13. H. Farrie, *Toiling Liverpool*, a series of articles printed by the Liverpool Daily Post from 8 to 19 March 1886.

14. W. Grisewood, *Poor of Liverpool*, A collection of pamphlets 1883-1905.

15. Rowntree and Sherwell. The temperance problem and social reform (London 1899) p. 15. Cited in J. Brown's article , the Pig or the Stye, *International Review of Social History, 1973*, p. 382.

16. Nathaniel Smyth, *Maps Showing the Licensed Premises in Liverpool 1875*. Police Register Reports included.

17. *Report from the Select Committee of the House of Lords on Intemperance*. Appendix Session 1878-79. p. xxxv.

18. *The Porcupine*, 14 February 1863.

19. Report on Intemperance, op. cit., p. xxxv.

Chapter Three

'THE PREVALENCE OF CASUAL LABOUR'

"There is probably no city of anything like equal size in which so small a proportion of the population is maintained by permanent and stable industrial work—the principle occupation of the city and the foundation of its prosperity is the handling of goods between ship, warehouse and railway; a function which is mainly performed by unskilled labour".[1]

Of all the causes of poverty and hardship in nineteenth century Liverpool, casualism, the most degrading as well as the most insecure form of employment, would be, perhaps, the major contributor in condemning countless souls to the lowest depths of deprivation. For the majority of casual labourers the overwhelming characteristic of working at the dockside or building site was the perennial struggle against poverty which derived from irregular employment. As Eric Taplin has argued, the efforts of a small number of the enlightened middle-class in exposing the iniquities of the casual system were nullified by the indifference of the majority of the employers of labour.[2] Just as the fortunes of some builders and landowners were made from the court and cellar dwellings, the fortunes of great shipping magnates, such as Cunard, Ismay and Brocklebank, were made by their exploitation of the casual system.

Casualism had developed at the docks from the twin factors of unpredictable labour demand and a glutted supply of labour. Demand essentially fluctuated according to cyclical, seasonal and local factors. The swings of the trade cycle were always likely to affect the volume of trade passing through the port and this was aggravated by the fact that the flow of goods was not evenly spread throughout the year, significant seasonal fluctuation being the norm. For example, the raw cotton crop reached Liverpool around October, and from October to the following April, as cotton poured into the port, the demand for labour rose. Yet once the cotton season ended work would become increasingly difficult to find. Local factors were important also. In the earlier part of our period, when sailing ships crossed the oceans of the world, vagaries of winds, and storms would affect employment. When a favourable West wind blew bouts of concentrated employment, involving long hours of work, could be expected. But when an adverse East wind, or exceptionally bad weather arose, vessels were prevented from entering or leaving port and periods of idleness and unemployment resulted.

No. 8 *Men unloading a cart. North west corner of Canning Dock c. 1890.* Photograph by C.F. Inston.

By the 1870's however, steam was increasingly replacing sail and with the fortunes of the weather eliminated one may have expected a more stable and permanent labour market to emerge. But almost the opposite actually occurred. The casual nature of waterfront work was intensified by the intense competition amongst steamship companies who demanded a quick turn around in port, which would enable them to work their vessels to maximum efficiency. Thus, work now came in sudden bursts, and at high pressure (of course, working under high pressure made an already dangerous occupation even more hazardous) and periods of idleness alternated with periods of heavy labour.

Nevertheless, despite this background, there were very few occasions when supply did not exceed demand for labour and in fact, the over-supply of labour was encouraged by employers to ensure that a pool of labour was always available to cope with the emergencies of exceptionally busy periods. They were able to continue this course for the simple reason that, apart from a few exceptions, the work available was essentially unskilled. Moreover, employers were well aware of the fact that almost anyone could do the job, and of course, there were no barriers to entry such as apprenticeship. Therefore, the casuals job was never secure and as Gareth Stedman Jones has commented through

"the interminable struggle to get enough to eat, the precarious hold upon a marginal employment, the dreaded anticipation of hard winters, sickness, and old age, and the final and inevitable assumption into the workhouse"

the casual poor were "brought up to treat life with the fatalism of the gambler".[3]

With the city's wealth so dependent on trade, times of commercial distress could prove to be very detrimental to the whole urban economy. A. T. McCabe has completed a statistical study showing the sensitivity of Liverpool to the vagaries of trade. Periods of poor trade were accompanied by high mortality rates, suggesting an inverse correlation between the two. His findings reveal that 1872 and 1873, two of the three healthiest years were also the two most prosperous in terms of trade. Whereas 1866, a very poor year for trade, experienced the highest death rate. It would be folly, of course, to put the cause of high mortality rates down to the state of trade alone. Numerous other variables would need to be added to the equation before we could reach any concrete conclusions, but there does appear to be a marked connection.

In establishing the identity of the Liverpool poor the diversity encountered is somewhat bewildering. Describing the poor by occupation would be a considerable and unenviable, task. Yet it was exactly this task which Grisewood was prepared to undertake when he asked the simple question 'who, then, are the poor?' in his *Poor of Liverpool* pamphlets.[4] His findings have to be viewed with scepticism, as he does not disclose his method of enquiry but they do provide us with a basic insight into the occupations that were most susceptible to poverty.

Not surprisingly the majority were found in waterfront occupations. Grisewood maintained that "about one-fifth of the whole are drawn from the ranks of the casual labourers, chiefly dock labourers, including the wives and children who depend on them". These men were usually in demand when young and strong, but when middle-aged their strength for sustained labour,

No. 9 *Overhead railway at the Pier Head c. 1890.* Photography by C.F. Inston.

and thus their employability had diminished. Next, 'making about one-eighth of the whole, came the cotton and general porters who work in the various warehouses'. Grisewood puts their plight down to 'adverse winds and depression in trade which fluctuated their work'. Associated with the work at docks and warehouses was large class of clerks engaged in checking, weight taking, etc. and again these men were dependent on the seasonal aspects of work opportunities, and subject to the same uncertainty of work. He then identifies those men in the various building trades—the bricklayers, plasterers and painters—whose work, once again, was seasonal. However, he points out that the skilled men 'seem to get over the slack time, but the same cannot be said for their labourers'. (One must remember that Grisewood is categorising the poor solely by occupation and no mention is made of the aged, the long-term sick and disabled and widows, hence his figures have to be seen in this light).

However, a whole host of other, less obvious, occupations which paid the wages of bare subsistence, could be added to Grisewood's list. Occupations such as chip-sellers, rubbing-stone dealers, salt-heavers, fruit hawkers, cotton and oakum pickers, crossing sweepers among others, attracted casual fringes of varying dimensions. Liverpool's occupational structure was probably very narrow in comparison with other large towns, but we cannot disregard those numerous occupations at the very bottom of the labour market when seeking a connection between poverty and occupation.

No. 10 *Back of St. John's market, Liverpool city centre c. 1890.* Photograph by C.F. Inston.

Iain Taylor has argued that casualism, and the resulting periodic unemployment it caused, had the effect of 'institutionalising poverty'. Ways of life and behaviour were shaped by it (drink, crime etc.) and economic and social mechanisms adopted to it. In times of distress the pawnshop, for example, was the only way to keep out of the clutches of the dreaded Poor Law institutions. Often regarded as the 'saviour' of the poor, the pawnshop was an integral part of affairs in the poor community. The 129 pawnbrokers that existed in Liverpool in 1855, for example, took in an average of 50,000 pledges a week.[5] Anything and everything of any value would be pawned from a wedding ring down to bedding and even underclothes. Sixty per cent of the objects pawned, in this particular year, were worth less than five shillings, and slightly over sixty per cent of the articles were redeemed within a month (pledging Monday and redemption the following Saturday was very

25

common). But, obviously, the pawnshop served merely as a short-term palliative to what was a long-term problem—the problem of poverty derived from the low and irregular earnings of the casual labourer.

The casual worker was trapped in a vicious circle from which there was little chance of escape. Moreover, the hope that his children might free themselves from a casual environment was similarly remote. Stedman Jones maintains that the conditions which promoted casual labour in one generation reproduced it in the next. He continued:

"when the casual labourer married and had children, his real standard of living declined. With each extra child came an extra burden of expenditure without any chance of immediate recompense; and in the absence of effective contraception family size was often restricted only by mortality, and each child increased the necessity of the wife to work to make ends meet".

If a wife did work it would usually be in some lowly paid menial job such as street selling (e.g. fruit, fish, matches) domestic service, cleaning, cotton picking or perhaps needle work either at home, which would at least enable

No. 11 *Outside the fish market, Great Charlotte Street c. 1890.* Photograph by C.F. Inston.

her to be with the children so that they would be less liable to be neglected, or in the sweatshops of the clothing trade. Linda Grant has highlighted the exploitation of women in these sweatshops which provided the only manufacturing industry of any consequence for female workers in the late nineteenth century. Located mainly in the city centre in Lord Street, Bold Street and North John Street women worked in appalling conditions for pitifully low wages. Large stores and clothing shops cut costs by giving work to 'sweaters' who would employ as many piece workers as possible on a casual basis to get the work done quickly as possible and then discharge the women until the next batch of work became available.[6]

Under such circumstances there is no doubt that some women turned to prostitution in order to survive. The lot of one poor household who resided in the court dwellings of Thomas Street in the 1860's was related to investigators who were making enquiries on behalf of the *Porcupine*. A young girl in her mid-teens is the narrator of the account (presumably she was taking care of the children whilst the parent were away). In reply to a question from one of the investigators regarding the welfare of the family she replied:

> "A mother, father and six children live here, the father is a salt-heaver and gets pretty fair work; but he drinks all he earns very nearly and scarcely gives his wife anything to support the family. She has to go out cotton-picking when she can get it to do, and when that's slack she does whatever she can to get her children a bit to eat".[7]

Two points emerge from this account. Firstly, its clear that male casual labour was accompanied by precisely similar, albeit even more poorly paid, intermittent forms of employment for women. Their work was as casual and as insecure as the dockworkers. Moreover, Liverpool women were at a disadvantage compared to women in other Lancashire towns where there were employment opportunities in manufacturing industry, such as the cotton mill, for the type of work available to them was restricted. Secondly, we have a typical example of the intemperant father who was totally indifferent to his family obligations. The poverty stricken wife and children were probably in desperate need of support, yet they would almost certainly have been classed as an 'undeserving unit' by the charitable institutions of the day. With the father being employed with 'pretty fair of work' his drinking would be deemed as the cause of their suffering. This falls in lines with the Victorians' settled opinion of the father as the head of the household. Consequently, with all issues emanating from his actions, the wife and children would be forced to suffer the consequences of his selfish behaviour. There was no safety net to catch the innocent victims of such cruel circumstances.

No. 12 *Women selling old clothes and rags at Fox Street market c. 1895.*
Photograph by T. Burke.

When one takes into account the levels of drinking, how many families existed in similar circumstances? The salt-heavers family was by no means an isolated case. Throughout the period, more examples can be found in *Porcupine* and other contemporary sources, of neglected battered or deserted wives and children.

To conclude we can briefly sum up the major points as follows: it is clear that Liverpool's narrowly based occupational structure had fundamental effects on the town's economic and social life. Taylor has argued that the commonest wage rates were those of the unskilled labour force and these rates determined the prevailing standards of diet, accommodation and general living conditions, all of which in turn were directly related to the abysmal public health situation that existed in the poor community. The spasmodic demand for labour was a primary cause of poverty in the port. But it was also an over-abundant supply of new labour competing for work that maintained the casual labour system, with a good deal of help from the employers themselves, and these factors operated against any amelioration. The majority of the poor could be found in locations near to and in the occupations associated with the waterfront. And with Liverpool's wealth so dependent on trade and commercial interests evidence suggests that economic slump and periods of poor trade would have a very adverse effect on the standards of living of the poor. Finally, there were the problems of alcohol and their association with poverty. Drink was a major problem, yet it was not necessarily a cause of the condition of the poor. Rather one has to look to the appalling environmental conditions in the lower quarters of the city and their effect on the poor for a solution of the causes of intemperance.

NOTES AND REFERENCES

1. Ramsay Muir, *History of Liverpool*, (S.R. Publishers, 1970), p. 306.

2. Eric L. Taplin, 'Dock Labour at Liverpool'. *Lancashire and Cheshire Transactions*, No. 122, 1977, p. 152.

3. G. Stedman Jones, *Outcast London*. (Oxford University Press 1971), p. 342.

4. W. Grisewood, *The Poor of Liverpool and What It Has done For Them*, series of pamphlets 1883-1905. (Reprinted from Liverpool Mercury).

5. I. C. Taylor, '*Blackspot on the Mersey*', p. 93.
    The Borough's total of accepted pledges amounted to 557,493 in this particular year (1855). Often stores were ... 'chocked with unredeemed articles' ... Taylor '*Blackspot*', p. 89.

6. L. Grant, 'Womens Work and Trade Unionism in Liverpool 1890-1914' in *Bulletin of North West Labour History Society* No. 7, 1980-81.

7. *The Porcupine*, November 22nd 1862, Chapter II of 'The Mysteries of the Courts',—'Thomas Street'.

Chapter Four

THE DESERVING AND UNDESERVING POOR

"The office of liberality consisteth in giving with judgement".
Cicero

The Central Relief Society of Liverpool, on its establishment in 1863, stated clearly that its chief objective was:

"to provide the necessaries of life for deserving families who through sickness on the part of the breadwinner, lack of work or unavoidable misfortune of any kind, were in need of help".[1]

The crucial word in this passage is 'deserving', for the general aim of the activities of the CRS was to impose upon the life of the poor a system of sanctions and rewards which would convince them that there could be no escape from the miseries we described in the first part of this study except, that is, by self-help in the form of thrift, regularity and hard work. In times of emergency deserving families would qualify for temporary relief—chiefly in the form of food and fuel, as cash payments were rarely given—which would assist them through the crisis. But the 'undeserving' were simply cast aside. There was always the Poor Law to save them from starvation. Thus, organisations like the CRS and the COS in London, had no interest in a man whose 'condition is due to improvidence or thriftlessness, and there is no hope of being able to make him independent in the future'. Rather, their ideal client, Fraser suggests, was the person in whom 'the seed of self-help and independence could be nurtured'.[2]

It was with these ingrained opinions in mind that the charitable institutions of the second half of the nineteenth century firmly supported two basic propositions; firstly, that poverty was avoidable through personal initiative and was not the result or consequence of the social and economic system; and secondly, that the extent of poverty could be adequately dealt with by voluntary philanthropic effort, thus precluding the need for large-scale state intervention. They would adhere to these assertions right up to and indeed, in some cases, well into the twentieth century.[3] The emphasis placed on self-help and independence overpowered all else in this type of atmosphere. The result was that poor families who were often in direct need of support were passed over. What is certain is that by the turn of the century some of the most deprived areas in Liverpool were still experiencing the most appalling conditions of poverty. Statistics for the period 1900 to 1904 reveal that the average mortality rate nationally was down to 16.0 per 1,000. By contrast, Scotland and Exchange Wards in Liverpool experienced averages which were over twice the national rate viz. Scotland Ward, 32.4 per 1,000, and Exchange Ward even higher at 33.4 per 1,000. Infant mortality was particularly high in these two wards and records show that the national average was well exceeded in both. In fact in 1906 the deaths of children under five years of age amounted to 54.5 per cent of the total deaths in the Scotland division.[4]

Thus, if mortality rates were significant pointers to the extent of poverty, one can visualise the conditions that still existed in these areas. Housing remained poor with court dwellings in appreciable numbers, and employment continued to be distributed on a casual basis on the waterfront and in the sweatshop. Contrary to the opinions of the various charitable institutions, therefore, all the evidence pointed to the fact that the condition of the poor was a consequence of the social and economic system and, furthermore, over forty years of charitable effort had failed to ameliorate the dreadful conditions of poverty. Massive state aid was required. The general opinion regarding the causes of poverty was beginning to change. There was increasing acceptance that it was not moral failure that was to blame but the social system itself.

It seems likely that the position of the poorest members of Liverpool's community was not improved in any marked way from the inception of the 'torrent of charity' in the mid-century years right up to the end of the nineteenth century. It is against this background that the study now turns its attention to a detailed examination of the methods of the philanthropist and his institutions.

Charitable activity in Liverpool can be traced as far back as the early eighteenth century when the Reverend Robert Stythe and Bryan Blundell, a master mariner, opened the first really permanent charitable institution. This was the Blue Coat Hospital, established in 1709, which provided for the education of poor and orphaned children. Other less notable concerns such as the almshouses for sailors' widows in Hanover Street, were also founded in this period. But it is with the nineteenth century and the founding of three main charities—the Stranger's Friend Society, the District Provident Society and the Charitable Society, that we must begin our investigation. These three societies were the largest charitable bodies in the town and they would eventually come to provide the fundamental base of the CRS. One of the chief reasons why the CRS was establishd was to ensure against 'indiscriminate charity'. William Rathbone, one of the founder members, and a true

No.13 *Dr. Duncan first Public Health Officer.*

philanthropist who was one of the few men who seemed to fully understand the position of the poor, abhorred the waste of charitable support. He, more than anyone else, was instrumental in persuading the three charities to amalgamate and thus, in his own words, put 'method in the place of muddle'.[5] Charitable services had originated in the reaction of individuals to specific situations rather than in methodical planning, with the result that the work of some societies overlapped whilst there were gaps where no provision at all was made. Co-operation and joint action between the various societies before amalgamation was sadly lacking, and one had a situation where societies vied in open competition with each other for the subscriptions of donors. This caused what *Porcupine* satirically called 'trumpet blowing machinery'[6] to become undesirably common. Moreover, Rathbone pointed out that because of the lack of co-operation much abuse of charity had resulted, with mendacious individuals often applying for, and indeed getting, relief from three or four different charities at the same time. This was brought to light when a check was made on recommendation notes which revealed that, in several instances, three notes—one for each society—came forward in favour of the same person at the same time. This situation convinced the societies that amalgamation would be beneficial to the interests of both the recipient and the donor.

Rathbone had been interested in the whole question of poor relief and in 1867 he published a small book, with the title of *Social Duties*[7] in which he outlined his views on charity. Margaret Simey maintains that his attention centred upon the importance of persuading the wealthy to give their minds to the proper, and in the long run, the most profitable use of their wealth. He was convinced that a change of heart on the part of the rich, and the organisation of their benevolence towards the poor could remedy the social strains and resentments that the industrial revolution had caused. In effect, Simey goes on, 'he advocated a system of voluntary socialism', which would manifest in a twofold effort: 'to rouse the rich to a sense of their social duties and to work out sound methods whereby they could express their obligations. But Rathbone's plans were never put into operation. His election to Parliament in 1868 meant that his opportunities for playing an active part in local charitable effort were restricted, and this can only be viewed as an unfortunate occurrence for the poor. Rathbone was an ally they could ill afford to lose. His plea for basing the administration of charity upon the human relations between individual rich and poor seemed to be quickly forgotten. The rich for the most part continued to ignore any social obligaions, and when they did give to charity, they gave indiscriminately. Moreover, the CRS placed its emphasis on even more stringent enquiries into applicant's circumstances as the Society found itself constantly arguing with indignant subscribers as to the correct interpretation of their deserving and undeserving classifications. These more intensive enquiries increasingly earned the CRS the reputation of being even harsher than the Poor Law. Many members of the poor community would rather suffer in silence than bear the indignity of the Society's investigation into their affairs.

An example of the criticism that was levelled at the harshness of the Society's enquiries was provided by the Rev. H. Postance, who was one of Liverpool's leading Church of England ministers in the 1890's. He had this to say in a speech to the Liverpool Clerical Society:

"Relief of the poor is always a difficult matter, and the temptation at times is to give up the attempt altogether and to let other hands and hearts engage in this work—such for instance as the Committee of the CRS. That this would be attended with disastrous results, so far as the poor are concerned, I am convinced, for it is difficult to satisfy the members of the Committee that a case is eligible for their attention, and their visitors often times excel the Relieving Officers in their unnecessary painful enquiries."[8]

Apart from the CRS the other main charitable bodies were religious and the lack of confidence between the CRS and the religious bodies is plainly obvious by the tone of this quote. Postance, it seems, was prepared to wash his hands of the poor, but the alternative of the CRS Committee's monopoly of poor relief was too drastic to contemplate. A closer examination of the methods of distribution of alms for the poor by religious bodies also reveals glaring irregularities.

Canon A. Hume provides a very interesting account of the conditions of the distribution of alms to the poor in the various ecclesiastical districts of the Borough of Liverpool for the year 1858.[9] Breaking them down into sixteen districts, Hume endeavoured to indicate the regions of pauperism, and even more minutely tried to break it down street by street with the help of Poor Law Relieving Officers. Reckoning every ecclesiastical district in the same way and dividing the town into north and south by a line passing along Dale Street and Shaws Brow (William Brown Street), he gave an estimate of the percentage of pauperism in each district. His findings revealed that there were eleven districts in which there were no pauper streets. Yet in every one of these eleven districts people still spoke of the 'poor' in their midst, though there may not have been a single family within the limits of really desperate poverty. In these more prosperous districts appeals for the 'poor'—for their relief, their education and so on, were always liberally responded to, with sums of up to £100 per annum collected, but it was in these districts here aid was least required. On the other hand, districts which were in the direst need with countless 'pauper streets', collected a meagre pittance of £1 or so per annum at the offertory of the poor. Ironically, there was no crossing of boundaries in terms of transferring monies, and similarly, no centralised religious body to administer doles from one district to another. Thus, the district system in Liverpool tended to create·several distinct communities who jealously made sure their donations were used in their own locality. The following quotation from Hume puts the matter in its true perspective.

"The operation of cause and effect at present is somewhat like the following. In one district we shall designate (A), there are only two families who receive relief from the parish or union. In another district (B) there are eight hundred such families, a ratio of 1:400. But in District (A), the incumbent curate and church wardens have 84 of alms from the offertory to distribute annually; in District (B), they have only 30 shillings. Here the supply is in the ratio of 56:1. Taking pauperism and aid together therefore the wants of the poor are better supplied in (A) to (B) by more than 20,000 to 1 (400 x 56)... It is altogether an anomaly, and a crying evil in in a christian land, that two communities whose members dwell side by side... should in many respects be practically as wide apart as if they resided in two separate quarters of the globe".[10]

No. 14 *Women and children in dockland Liverpool c. 1890.* Photograph by C.F. Inston.

When considering the overall situation in both the private and religious bodies therefore, one tends to agree with David Owen who stressed the inefficiency, unimaginativeness and complete lack of originality of the nineteenth century charities. Yet for the Victorians the philanthropic societies were subjects of national pride. They often congratulated themselves on the scale of their charities which, Harrison suggests, were manifest in the numerous charity balls, philanthropic dinners and elegant membership cards of the societies. But money collected gave pleasure to some of the not so poor before it finally filtered down to those in real need. We have already noted (Chapter 1) examples of fraud, ambition, snobbery and the blatant use of charity for social mobility. On the whole the Victorian philanthropists' methods and characters are very easily criticised. Yet it was not all bad, it would be wrong to ignore the tireless work of some dedicated individuals in the charitable field in nineteenth century Liverpool.

William Rathbone VIth, his father William Vth his mother Elizabeth and daughter Eleanor would all occupy high places on any roll of honour. Eleanor, in particular, had inherited her father's most obvious qualities and Margaret Simey has pointed out that despite the handicaps and frustrations she encountered, simply because of her sex, she accomplished much sterling work on behalf of the poor community in Liverpool. 'That blend of principle and practice, that methodical marshalling of facts and resources, that profound and impartial philanthropy, which had characterised her father's approach to the problems of poverty in his day now reappeared in hers in relation to the problems of the early twentieth century' is how Simey describes her efforts. Then there were such outstanding men as the Rev. John Johns, a Devonian, who came to Liverpool on his appointment as 'Minister of the Poor' for the Domestic Mission in 1836 and was appalled at the levels of poverty he encountered. He quickly devoted his time and effort to combating poverty and destitution in the worst of the city centre slums, a labour which, tragically, he would pay for with his own life at the age of 46 when he contracted cholera in 1847. We could point to the small house in Great Howard Street in which every Saturday evening from the mid-1880's under the supervision of a Mr. R. C. Scott and a committee composed of labourers, a dock labourers relief fund was granted.[11] This body was prepared to listen to, and help, any cases of hardship, deserving or undeserving. Kitty Wilkinson, who in association with Elizabeth Rathbone was famous for opening the country's first public baths and wash-house, also did much voluntary work for the poor. During the time of the first cholera epidemic in 1832, she unselfishly opened her cellar as a wash-house for the clothing and bed-linen of cholera victims. Campaining journalist Hugh Shimmin of *Porcupine* fame frequently exposed the inadequacies of the Poor Law and the ineffeciencies of the charitable societies' methods in his editorials. H. Lee Jones founded the Food and the Betterment Association in 1893, the aim of which was, "To feed, clothe, shelter and cheer, those in need irrespective of need".[12] We can see that the struggle against poverty was not solely managed by the Committee of the CRS. Yet there can be no doubt that it was the latter's institutions which overwhelmingly presided over the administration of poor relief in the city, throughout the period.

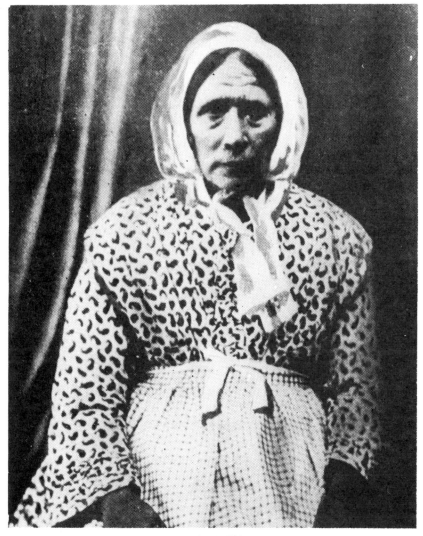

No. 15 *Kitty Wilkinson*

By the 1890's Grisewood was proudly boasting that there were now several hospitals in the city which were run by charitable organisations. He then went to great pains and into much detail, to describe the various 'Charities of Liverpool' as they were in the 1890's. As well as the hospitals he listed institutions for the blind, deaf and dumb, orphanages, a Society for the Prevention of Cruelty to Children, day nurseries, three houses for lodging, and the provision of work for youths who were 'adrift and without proper homes', no less than five institutions for the care of young women and girls who needed 'training and protection', homes for aged seamen, various almshouses provided for the shelter of widows and the aged, and several societies promoting temperance. An impressive list by any account, but nevertheless they merely scratched the surface of the problem of chronic poverty in the city. There was still little provision for the amelioration of the root causes of poverty. Important areas such as housing, employment, public health and education continued to be denied the proper attention they so desperately required.

An examination of some of the CRS's policies, particularly on employment, reveals the lack of originality, and, at times, the sheer futility of some of their efforts on these questions. Writing in 1899, Grisewood revealed that over the past 28 years the Society had assisted 2,050 persons to move from the 'poverty and hardship of Liverpool to the independence and comfort of elsewhere'. In fact, the majority were sent to the factory districts of Lancashire and Yorkshire where, realistically, 'comfort' was very hard to find. He goes on to suggest that the removal of over 2,000 persons to factories may be claimed as not only benefiting those who left, but, by 'lessening the competition for work here—those who also remained behind'. Furthermore, many of those sent away were in receipt of parish relief and therefore, he says, 'the relief to the rates has been considerable'. Clearly this policy had little real impact. Even if the relocation did benefit the migrants, when one takes into account that these 2,000 relocations were spread over a twenty-eight year period, and that the population of Liverpool at this time stood at approximately 700,000, the policy could have had little or no impact on the overall levels of poverty. On the question of dock labour and its casual nature, Grisewood advocated the principle of permanent contract instead of temporary. He goes on to suggest that:

"If there should still prove to be a surplus of labour over ordinary requirements, when a period of activity of trade has passed away, it might be well to consider the question of facilitating the emigration of suitable men to the colonies".[13]

It seems as though Grisewood was in favour of initiating some sort of 'charitable Tolpuddle' amongst the labourers of Liverpool to remedy possible unemployment. He seems to have been heavily influenced by the writings of Thomas Carlyle, the Scottish essayist and historian, on this particular point. Grisewood describes Carlyle, who had published a number of criticisms of economic and social conditions in industrial England, as "a man who had a wonderful insight into economic truth".

The point was that signs of progress on the relief of chronic poverty were less than forthcoming and, what is more, the Committee were becoming increasingly aware of the fact. Just before the end of the century, therefore, with the dual purpose of reconsidering both their own position and that of the poor, the Committee, through Grisewood, stated that

"In order to effect any improvement in the condition of the poor it is essential to have a correct idea as to what their condition actually is, and what are the causes that have produced it, whether external to themselves, or arising from faults or weaknesses in their own character".[14]

The Committee accordingly issued to their Voluntary Friendly Visitors forms containing a series of questions of these points. The personal feelings of the Visitors, as might be expected, counted for a good deal in many of the answers and this point should not be overlooked. For example, some Visitors were most impressed with the need of getting rid of the evil of drink, while others looked rather to an improvement in the dwellings and general surroundings of the poor for amelioration of their condition. The first two questions on the form merely related to the streets and trades of which the informant was enquiring. The third question asked, 'to what do you ascribe principally the distress in your section during the last six months?', and the answers were classified as follows:

Answers	Number of times named
General irregularity of work (especially for dock labour) and temporary slackness	30
Intemperance	21
Sickness	19
Improvidence	11
Indolence	11
Winter and season slackness	5
Vice and evil habits	3

Additionally, the following causes were named once: old age, weakness, accident, misfortune, foreign competition, depression, piece-work, over-population, strangers coming to Liverpool for work, large family, early marriage, incompetence, carelessness and independence at work.[15]

Irregularity of work occupies first position, but three out of the next four classifications are occupied by what would have been classed as 'avoidable' causes, intemperance, improvidence and indolence, and they figure prominently in other questions on the form.

Question four, for example, asked what 'the causes of irregularity of work were and what remedies could be suggested?' Respondents gave the principal causes as:

Answers	Number of times named
Overstocked labour market (especially in regard to dock labour)	9
Intemperance	5
Indolence	4
Strangers coming to Liverpool to seek work	2
Season trades	2
(Various other single causes were given).	

.As may be anticipated from the causes itemised, there were several different remedies proposed, including the regulation of dock labour in order to secure regular and continuous employment for as many men as possible, and the reduction of stands for hiring men on the line of docks. However, it was noted that the securing of constant employment to some who were irregular would have the effect of throwing others entirely out of work. What did the Committee propose should be done with these men? The answer was familiar: 'provision would be needed to assist these persons to migrate to other parts of the country, or emigrate to the colonies'.[16]

Once again, intemperence and indolence occupy high places in the causes of irregularity of work. Grisewood identified the plight of one wretched family which, presumably, he himself visited:

"Here for instance is a man who goes out delivering circulars three days a week getting 2/6 a day. The remaining three days he sits at home having no energy to look for work. His children run about almost naked. His wife lies ill on the vermin covered mattress without any bedclothes. Intemperence, indolence and sheer indifference to family obligations are at the root of this misery and it is sheer folly, if not worse, to treat it as a case of simple poverty and administer palliatives in the shape of charitable gifts".[17]

No. 16 *Local women and children on the corner of Prince Edwin Lane and Beresford Street.*

Obviously, this family was in desperate need of support but would receive none because the cause was seen as 'undeserving'. It was with this kind of situation in mind that question six was framed with a view to elicit practical remedies for "intemperance and idleness". In regard to intemperance, several visitors replied that they could propose no fresh remedies, and one visitor stated that 'there were in certain streets, several families always drunk from Saturday to Tuesday, and the children on the run every half-hour for beer and gin mixed'. However, although no radical remedies were suggested others were in favour of giving old remedies a full and fair trial. Suggestions included Sunday closing, prohibition of children being served, and the establishment of reading rooms in close proximity to the poor districts. Other alternatives went to the opposite extremes when one visitor was moved to say that 'intemperance is often a disease and should be so treated. Shut the victim up'. The brewers would undoubtedly have had something to say in regard to the former proposals. Whilst surely even the most heartless members of the Committee would not abide by the latter.

Question twelve inquired if there were many instances of "improvident or early marriage", the implication being that such marriages were amongst the most fruitful causes of distress. One visitor remarked that several girls were married at sixteen, and noted one man of twenty-four with six children. Grisewood visited a young couple in a north end court situated in Virgil Street off Cazaneu Street. He describes specifically how early and improvident marriage could lay the foundation for a typical pauper family. However, the conversation between Grisewood and the husband illustrates many of the points made in response to other questions on the form. The husband was eighteen and his wife seventeen, they, had been married for eight months.

Grisewood:	Are you in work?
Husband:	Not regular.
Grisewood:	What is your occupation?
Husband:	Carrying parcels at St. John's Market— just odd jobs.
Grisewood:	What do you earn?
Husband:	Ten to twelve shillings a week.
Grisewood:	What does your wife do?
Husband:	She goes out with a basket selling fish or fruit.
Grisewood:	Why did you marry young and with so little means?

42

Husband:	Well, I had no parents and no home and her stepmother wasn't kind to her and we thought we would get married and have a place of our own.
Grisewood:	Had you any furniture?
Husband:	Yes. What you see here.

Grisewood describes a three-legged table, an old chair or two, a dirty mattress, no bedclothes, no bedstead and a few bits of crockery.

Husband:	We bought them from a woman whose house we took over for 7/6.
Grisewood:	Where did you get the 7/6.
Husband:	It was what I earned that week.
Grisewood:	You have changed your address recently from No. 5 Court?
Husband:	Yes, that house had a stone floor and it was cold for my wife (looking down at her shoeless feet); she was feeling ill and so we came here where there is a wooden floor.[18]

This conversation highlights an earlier point made by Gareth Steadman Jones (Chapter Three) where he maintained that the casual labourer was trapped in a vicious circle. From such a bad start there would be little chance of escape from poverty for this young couple. Perhaps the only respite from such circumstances would ultimately be found in the public house.

The final question asked was, "Can you suggest any steps for the improvement of the condition of the poor generally?" Here there were some quite radical proposals put forward by the visitors, but by a distinct minority. The majority emphasised drink as the major problem, fortifying the theme of moral failure. Another suggested a rather topical remedy today 'the provision of more open spaces, and the planting of trees in the poorer quarters'. But other proposals included the introduction of a system of old age pensions, and one enlightened Visitor proposed that the State should take oversight of every child to secure its proper support, education and training.

As far as can be ascertained however, on the results of this enquiry, most of the visitors were devoid of new ideas for the amelioration of poverty in their relief work, and it leads one to ask whether the CRS visitors could ever really understand the poor, or indeed, in turn be understood by them. After all, they would have been on two vastly different social planes. The majority of

No. 17 *Barefoot women in a Liverpool street. c. 1895.* Photograph by T. Burke.

Friendly Visitors came from middle class backgrounds. Simey has pointed out that, as far as is known, the CRS never appointed any member of the working classes to any of its Committees and all in all this can only have been detrimental to the fortunes of the Liverpool poor.

By 1902 signs that opinions were changing were becoming more evident.

Some of the district Committees of the CRS were beginning to protest against the Society's methods. In one case the Toxteth Committee argued, in its annual report of that year, that

"The drink question, the labour question, and the housing question seem to stand in the way of all attempts to deal effectively with distress, and as years go on certain members of the Committee feel more and more strongly the inadequacy and superficiality of much of their work of relief".[19]

No doubt Eleanor Rathbone, a member of this particular Committee, was one who shared these doubts. These cross currents within the Society presented what was, in fact, the first real threat to the original principles of organised charity that had been preached by the CRS for nearly forty years. It was beginning to be argued that a revision or reinterpretation of the rules concerning the 'deserving' and 'undeserving' classifications was long overdue. But old habits die hard, and as Simey argues, being loyal to the traditions of their founders the CRS were loath to change. This was plainly evident when they invited Mr. A. Mercer who was Secretary of the Blackburn Charity Organisation (COS) to address the Annual Conference of Friendly Visitors (1904) on the subject of "Charity and Family Responsibility". It seems Mercer was a member of the 'old school' in that he advocated all the old principles of self-help and individualism when he stated that the only way to make charity effective was to first

"try to develop self-help; then to obtain the help of relatives; and after that of friends, neighbours and employers. It is not till these 'natural' sources are exhausted that we should look to the church or other charitable funds; and if all else is insufficient to the benevolence of donors in a better position".[20]

Ironically Mercer was absolutely correct in some respects. For where had the myriad of 'undeserving' been finding relief for all those years if the CRS and others were not prepared to give any? William Rathbone had no doubts: 'these sufferers were cared for by their own brethren and neighbours'.[21] There were many examples of working class communities clubbing together to help families through a crisis. Terence Cooke maintains that there was certain clanishness in the communities. Relatives often lived close to one another and they would help each other financially in hard times. Friends and neighbours could also contribute to the community spirit. If, for instance, illness struck down the mother of a family, neighbours would often tend children, provide meals and do cleaning and washing.

However, it was the final indignity of the paupers grave which was feared most by the poor. A few coppers were usually put aside each week with a

Burial Society or tontine, to provide for a decent funderal. Unfortunately, not every society was efficiently managed and some were dishonestly conducted. There were instances of fraud and deception amongst collectors and secretaries, which led *Porcupine* to expose what it called the 'Burial Society humbug'.[22] In a case of insolvency, be it by fraud or mismanagement, the deceased family would need to revert to the means which Mercer highlighted; 'natural sources' in the form of street and/or pub collections to provide the money for the burial. It is clear that if this moral and financial support had been denied in times of direst need, many more pauper funerals would have taken place.

As it was Mercer's speech has to be seen as something of a swan-song. Nationally the reports of Charles Booth and Seebohm Rowntree on poverty in London and York respectively had been published. They had investigated poverty in a scientific and rational manner and their conclusions came as a great shock to many middle-class observers. They argued that povety was widespread in the typical Victorian city, with up to a third of the urban population living below the poverty line. When one takes into account the fact that, at the corresponding time, Poor Law officials were talking in terms of only two or three per cent. of people in England Wales in receipt of Poor Law relief, the shock was quite understandable. Rowntree's concepts of primary poverty, where earnings were below subsistence, secondary poverty, where earnings were above subsistence but expenditure was wasteful, and his notion of the poverty cycle, where the individual went through cycles of poverty throughout his life in times of unemployment, sickness, or lay-off, were especially influential in changing people's attitudes.

At the same time the working class itself was becoming increasingly organised and articulate. The rise of socialism with the emergence of the Social Democratic Federation in the 1880's and the founding of the Independent Labour Party in the 1890's meant that the working class voice was becoming increasingly audible. Both organisations were active in Liverpool and tried to highlight the plight of the poor in meetings and rallies held in places like St. George's Plateau and the Wellington Monument. One notable sight that could be seen once a week on St. George's Plateau in the 1890's which was run jointly by the SDF, the ILP and the Fabian society was the "Clarion Van", which provided bread and soup for the poor whilst it was parked on the forecourt of the noble Hall. Added to this was the emergence of the "New Unionism" of the unskilled worker, which manifested itself in Liverpool for the first time with the dockers strike of 1890. Moreover, the extension of the franchise in 1884, which incrased the nation's electorate by two million voters, many of whom were working class, ensured that the problems of the low paid and the casually employed were not going to be so

No. 18 *Liverpool rag pickers at New Brighton. This annual treat was provided by Lee Jones' League of Welldoers.*

easily swept under the carpet. The notion that poverty was self-inflicted had waned considerably by the early twentieth century and even advocates of temperance were now willing to admit to the widespread existence of economic poverty, i.e. poverty caused through no moral fault of the person involved.

In Liverpool, Owen has stressed that during the last years of the nineteenth century it is 'impossible to miss amid the self-congratulation and official optimism of the Annual Reports a note of disappointment that the CRS formula had not effected a more revolutionary improvement in the life of the poor'. Members of the Society knew that they were fighting a battle they could never hope to win. Their efforts had not succeeded in reducing the volume of poverty and suffering as the conditions of Scotland, Exchange and Vauxhall Wards testified and by the second decade of the twentieth century they were resigned to the fact that only state legislation on social policy could provide an effective answer.

Owen maintains that by the early 1920's the Society had plainly lost its momentum. The Liverpool Council of Voluntary Aid, a by-product of the

Royal Commission on the Poor Laws which had been set up in 1905, gradually took over the position that the CRS occupied in the second half of the nineteenth century. Finally, in 1932, the Central Relief Society was itself absorbed into the City Council. Men of such diverse characters as Rathbone and Grisewood had passed through the Society's ranks in its seventy-year history, many different charities had come under its umbrella, and undoubtedly many hundreds of lives had been saved. How many more could have been saved by an early change in the "deserving" and "undeserving" distinction enforced by the Society is a question which can only remain open to argument.

NOTES AND REFERENCES

1. W. Grisewood, *The Poor of Liverpool*, and *What is done*, p. 31.

2. Fraser, *'Welfare State'*, p. 122.

3. See note 20, Mr. A. Mercer's speech in 1904.

4. Infant Mortality; 1901-1905

	National average	138/1000
	Scotland ward	229/1000
	Exchange ward	244/1000

   M.O.H. Annual Report 1905 in *Council Proceedings 1905/6* pp. 1149-1154.
   See also; Dr. Hugh Jones, *Medico-Chirurgical Journal 1909* pp. 101-102.

5. He summed up his conclusions in regard to charity in a small book which he originally called 'Method versus muddle in Charitable Work', but he changed the name later to Social Duties (see note 10).

6. *The Porcupine*, 27 January 1866. Quoted in Simey, *'Charitable Effort'*, p. 83.

7. Full title was *'Social Duties, considered in Reference to the Organisation of Effort in Works of Benevolence and Public Utility'*.

8. The speech was on the subject of—*'The difficulties of pastoral and Educational Works in Poor Parishes'*. (Read before the Liverpool Clerical Society; Liverpool 1884). Reverend H. Postance. Cited in A.T. McCabe, *Standard of Living on Merseyside 1830-75*, p. 191.

9. Canon A. Hume, *Conditions of Liverpool, analysis of the Present Population*. Chapter 1, Part VII, p. 20.

10. Hume, *'Condition of Liverpool'*, p. 23.

11. Scott and his committee were highlighted by H. Farrie in his articles *'Toiling Liverpool'*—Liverpool Daily Post March 8 - 19th 1886. The fund had started with a capital of £5.

12. See Terence Cooke, *Scotland Road, The Old Neighbourhood* p. 28. (Countyvise 1987).

13. Grisewood, *'Poor of Liverpool'*, p. 43.

14. W. Grisewood, The Poor of Liverpool. *Notes on their Condition*—based on an enquiry made by the Liverpool Central Relief Society, p. 3.

15-18 Grisewood, *'Poor of Liverpool'*, pp. 5-16.

19. CRS, Toxteth District Committee *Annual Report 1902*. Quoted in Simey *'Charitable Effort'*, p. 137.

20. A. Mercer, *'Charity and Family Responsibility'*, A paper read at the Annual Conference of Friendly visitors, October 20th 1904.

21. W. Rathbone, *The Organisation of Charity*, A letter from Rathbone, January 1887. Liverpool Record Office. H. 361. RAT.

22. See *Porcupine* volume 2. 1861 p. 294-295 and volume 4. 1862-63 p. 378 for full description and criticism of Burial Societies in Liverpool.

23. J. Brown, 'The Pig or the Stye', an article in the *International Review of Social History*, 1973, p. 393.

Chapter Five

CONCLUSION

It is clear that a great amount of work would be involved in a full and comprehensive study of the subjects in this book. Poverty and philanthropy in Victorian Britain is a huge area and in Liverpool alone the problem was vast. I only claim to have covered a chapter of what would be a huge literary volume. However, what I have tried to do is illustrate the primary features and causes of poverty in Liverpool and identify the methods and attitudes of the most important individuals and institutions who concerned themselves with philanthropy. In arranging the composition of the study it was not my intention to simply present a narrative account of the charitable bodies and the way they related to the poor of Victorian Liverpool. Essentially, my intention was to present an analytical study of both and elucidate the relationship between the two.

What brief conclusions can be reached therefore? The overall argument of this study has certainly been critical of the charitable institutions, and in particular the Central Relief Society, in the city. Individuals such as William and Eleanor Rathbone and the Rev. John Johns achieved some outstanding work on behalf of the poor, but it is most important to distinguish between the motives and actions of people like the Rathbones and those of the men and women at 'grass roots' level i.e. the Voluntary Friendly Visitors and the actual donors themselves. We have seen, given the prevailing sentiments that were expressed in the answers to the CRS Committee's questionnaires, that the majority of Visitors thought poverty to be the result of moral failure on the part of the poor. But then one could further argue, perhaps, that the Visitors had been indoctrinated by the principles of the Society itself, which emphasised that only deserving cases should qualify for relief. Grisewood put it perfectly:

"It was properly pointed out by a Visitor that chronic and constantly recurring cases of distress are not suitable for the aid of the Society, which seeks rather to take in hand those who can be assisted to permanent self-support".[1]

Nevertheless, having said that, one would still not deny the constructive purposes that inspired the formation of the Central Relief Society in 1863.[2]

Something did have to be done in regard to both indiscriminate charity within the field of charitable relief in the early part of our period. But were the enquiries carried out by the Society's investigators too stringent? At times it seems, the detection of the mendacious individual, or as Grisewood once called them 'these illegitimate beggars', became something of an obsession. From a speech delivered to the Myrtle Street Literacy and Debating Society in 1895[3] one gets the distinct impression that Grisewood was more concerned with avoiding the possibility of giving relief to the mendacious and undeserving than he was of administering relief to the Society's deserving cases. Central to this argument was the familiar spectre of moral failure which manifested itself in alcohol, improvidence and idleness. The poverty of the poor was intrinsically associated with these failings and they were seen as causes and not symptoms of their condition. I can find no evidence to suggest that Grisewood wavered from this position in his time in office.[4]

It is clear that the theme of moral failure as the cause of poverty preceded all else in the Victorian period, and Liverpool was no exception to the rule. Yet as early as the 1840's Dr. Duncan had stated fearlessly that 'the wretchedness of the poor was the consequence of their circumstances and necessarily their own fault'.[5] And, Rathbone in a letter he wrote in 1887 also maintained that:

"A great deal of poverty is the result of vice and drunkenness. But this does not in any way relieve us from the obligation, whether as Christians or men, of dealing with this matter, for we are undoubtedly responsible for much of that drunkenness through our neglect in time past to provide the people with the power to obtain and enjoy more cultivated pleasures than those of the public house".[6]

Duncan recognised the total inadequacy of the environment of the poor and Rathbone acknowledged the social obligations of the 'better off' and the need to stress their 'social duties'. Yet overall, both Duncan's and Rathbone's observations were sadly neglected. Nineteenth century Liverpudlian philanthropic opinion overwhelmingly believed in the reformation of the individual and not in the glaring deficiencies of the surrounding environment. And generally, as far as social obligations were concerned, it seems the majority of the better off proportion of the Liverpool public did little more than ostracise the poor community and leave them to their own destiny. As *Porcupine* put it in 1867:

"There are people among us who never fail in their Christian duty...but then these generous and energetic persons are not many. They are as nothing when compared with those who do nothing—who never give to any charity—never exert themselves in any good cause. The bulk of the Liverpool public is a solid, inert, almost insoluble mass, not warmed or melted by any impulse or any sunny ray of charity. It does not occur to them to do anything: it does not seem any part of their business. The really beneficient workers of Liverpool are always hot as the three hundred spartans in the gap—the three Romans on the bridge . . . ".[7]

A lot of water has passed under the bridge since. Yet all the past sufferings of the poor in Liverpool were perhaps not without some good effect for their misery was the spur which made Liverpool a cradle of the social services of the modern Welfare State.[8] One thing is certain, the "bad old days" will not be forgotten. Perhaps the best remaining evidence of the deplorable conditions which existed in Victorian Liverpool is kept in the various street names of the lower quarters of the city. Many still survive, and they are, for me, a constant physical reminder of the poverty and destitution they once harboured. Streets such as Fontenoy Street, Henry Edward Street, Addison Street, Preston Street, (Sir) Thomas Street and Hockenhall Alley are just a few. All are less than half a mile from the splendid Victorian architecture of St. George's Hall. They might well have been located, to use Canon Hume's phrase "in two separate quarters of the globe".

NOTES AND REFERENCES

1. Grisewood, *'Poor of Liverpool, Notes on Their Condition'*, p. 24.

2. D. Owen, *'English Philanthropy'*, p. 465.

3. W. Grisewood, How to Cope with Winter Distress, paper read to Myrtle Street Literary and Debating Society, November 11th, 1895.

4. Grisewood was a chartered accountant by profession. Born in Whitehaven in 1845, he became Secretary of the CRS in 1871 at the remarkably young age of 26. He died in 1915 aged 70 and by all accounts he still occupied the office of Secretary at the time. He was, certainly, still Secretary of the Society in 1911, according to W. T. Pikes Contemporary Biographies published that year.

5. Quote cited in Chandler *'Liverpool'*, p. 410. Taken from Liverpool Domestic Mission Annual Report 1847.

6. W. Rathbone, The Organisation of Charity, a letter 1887.

7. *The Porcupine*, 9th January 1867, quoted in Simey *'Charitable Effort'*, p. 82.

8. Chandler, *'Liverpool'*, p. 417.

Suggested further reading

Asa Briggs, *Victorian People*, Penguin, 1970.

Terence Cook, *Scotland Road, The Old Neighbourhood*, Countyvise 1987.

Derek Fraser, *The Evolution of the British Welfare State: A History of Social Policy Since the Industrial Revolution*, Macmillan, 1984.

M. E. Rose, *Relief of Poverty 1834-1914*, Macdonald, 1972.

E. L. Taplin, *Liverpool dockers and Seamen 1870-1890*, Hull University Press, 1974.